Two Notes for Home

for Seán and Matthew

Terry McDonagh

TWO NOTES FOR HOME

Two Notes for Home

is published in 2022 by
ARLEN HOUSE
42 Grange Abbey Road
Baldoyle
Dublin D13 A0F3
Ireland
Email: arlenhouse@gmail.com
www.arlenhouse.ie

ISBN 978–1–85132–293–0, paperback

International distribution
SYRACUSE UNIVERSITY PRESS
621 Skytop Road, Suite 110
Syracuse
New York 13244–5290
USA
Email: supress@syr.edu
www.syracuseuniversitypress.syr.edu

Typesetting by Arlen House

Cover image by Sally McKenna
is reproduced courtesy of the artist

CONTENTS

Two Notes for Home

Introduction

Poetry is the past that breaks out in our hearts
– Rainer Maria Rilke

There's something about the word home *that breaks out in our hearts.* Chant it and it resonates like *om* – a sacred sound and spiritual symbol. Home captures and pulls us back to something fundamental and indefinable that has little to do with physical place. Home is a matter of the heart. *Om* is a matter of the heart.

In *Two Notes for Home,* I'm caught between the sounds of two places. I like the sound of Mayo. I like the sound of Hamburg. They are *om* sounds but the bricks and mortar in Hamburg and the bricks and mortar in Mayo could not have constituted a home without people filling them with soul. In essence, they are cosy postal addresses with the potential to become a home. I have two of them.

Two Notes for Home

All season long the young man
lay on a riverbank
listening to proud cuckoos
chanting notes in twos
as cuckoo partners
dropped an egg here and there
to keep the line alive.
Good on ye, birds, he whispered
wistfully turning the page.

But when strawberries and sun
lost sight of each other
and Fibby the feline rambled off
to self-cater, he pulled
his designer t-shirt from the pile,
oiled and stroked his considerable mane
and set an alarm clock for the first time.

The bus would be passing in a while
so he took leave of his high horse,
tied himself in knots as best he could
and fled out of step without sweeping
the dance floor – it wasn't his to sweep.

He was in no hurry to arrive, but
once there, he tossed his backpack
to homestay, unveiled the espresso pot,
put sleep to one side – relishing a life
of dark silhouettes, trashy goings on
and the twinkle of blue and red barstools …

and the pizza place
at the opera house corner

was a gush of joy –
the best Italian ever!

Time passed as it must and one evening,
watching his dreams skim the river,
he began to think of dead poets, songs
to the gods and all that. Not there yet
but he'd published overseas, bought
a tweed jacket and learned to bump
about in figures of eight until his entire self
started to tire of city drills and melancholy.

To hell with conformity. Time withers,
and later will be too late, echoed up
from deep down where the heart is.

In panic, he flung his footwear to the wind
and rambled about barefoot until
his feet wore thin aching for solid,
when a voice like a foghorn
called out: *Your time has come, Mr Alter Ego.*

He'd been flying headlong into headlights
on a wing and a prayer – with baggage
and questions that worked on each other.
That was it. Adieu, Ciao, Tschuess, Cheerio.

With twittering and curtain calls done
he was ready to return
to where his high horse intoned
there's no place like home
in an upper room – to where
bewitchery, tomfoolery and loose ends
danced like cobwebs in moonlight.

He rocked up with a can of fresh paint,
a shed full of shiny garden tools
and a few litres of continental beverages.

He does hear a cuckoo airing notes
in twos – but home is a single note.
And it's enough.

The Plain of the Yew Trees or County Mayo

If this county of Saint Colman was flat,
we'd be stuck for words but it's not –
anything but. There are hilltops that

chieftains perched upon and a mountain
where Saint Patrick mused and ordered
snakes to take their hollow hiss elsewhere.

His shadow still hovers as we flutter
like butterflies around a prima donna
or apprentice peacocks at farmyard parties.

If you can trust the rumour mill,
a few flaky folk, drunk on dread
in dodgy tracksuits, are tethered

to telegraph wires with one ear on
railway sleepers hoping to pick up
on whom is next in line for favours.

Some newlyweds worry about carpet colour
or the purr of love in remote regions while
others trend in carbon-free dating on a grand scale.

One August afternoon I shared the base of
a dreamy beech with marauding midges
while reflecting on rhythm and rip roaring,

and later that evening, eavesdropping with
a lively Merlot as companion, I tuned
into faces as lost as mayflies in October.

Now I ask, if there be a god, he or she
must be amused at our blush and bluster
in that slim corridor of day and dark.

Monks in monasteries sprinkled some solace
by opening doors to a remote heaven until
they were defiled by outlandish pillage.

It seems that offering the other cheek or
sanctuary in sainthood was no solution either.
Hungry people died on doorsteps as their

horizon sank to its knees. Those who could
took off in tall ships singing of godsend
or praying as homeland buckled and faded.

As a child I was a lone hero in charge of
a nation's fortunes in hail, sunshine,
hard of heart and humpty dumpty off the wall.

There were forests too. I had one all to myself,
not huge, but enough for a jungle of wildlife
and brambles that snared me into their ensemble.

New trees grew out of old trees. Clouds were
debris in wind and water found its way when
hyperventilating machines were as foreign as

dignitaries flip-flopping at functions. History
was slow to begin but there were legends in
bogs and hilltops long before ring-fenced doctrine

kept us in place – before politicians followed
funerals in finery. I know because I'm of this
rough and tumble landscape – this table talk

of legend and ritual. I listened to spirits
around gravestones in Cill Aodáin and
doctrine in Roman churches. My ancestors

shared hilltop chant with haws and batwing magic
but when I tried to mesh a heavenly paradise
with the ancient coastline from Killary fjord to

the River Moy estuary they refused to budge,
so I turned back to the song and chant of
a black breeze in old, earthy, pagan ways.

Some soulful songs are not sung anymore,
but I know that, if we listen, they're still there
in the silence of raw, half-forgotten bogland.

The Right to Speak

I'm not muddled nor am I without sleep when I say
I came to Hamburg in the eighties like a
half-baked alien full of mischief and light-headedness.

I'd wanted to slip in and out of my own ego – be
in a storybook – get lost and tangle about like
a fistful of feathers in a vortex of my own making.

It was about discovery – no longing, no life. Shoots
pop up when you least expect. John Lennon said:
I was born in Liverpool but grew up in Hamburg.

I sharpened my pencil. The city gave me the right
to speak – to own up to the injured wolf in me – to
journey through a landscape of dykes that keep water

from losing the run of itself. It's a city on piling that
boasts of landmarks, erotica and merchant families.
Johannes Brahms and Heinrich Heine lived here too.

I wove my pen into the rich fabric and flare of the
edgy streets while the North Sea, beyond, rolled in
and out shaping its coastline without rock or clock.

At low tide and calm, we could walk the mud flats
to an island, but when storms do strike, trees gasp
and walls of sand are tossed from one corner to another

helpless as weak resolve. If this was an Irish set, I'd
have a dreamlife of hills and mountain ranges as guides,
but here slopes have to be imagined or learnt by heart.

I was an Icarus with a street view of scraps and words in cobwebbed alleyways – while hanging between fire and water in the raging racket of life.

There were statues that looked like gods and some that looked like stone. Hamburg had laid hands on me and I was able to shed old cold icons and have my say.

AUF WIEDERSEHEN HAMBURG

I'd found it hard to knock on doors back then.
It was all new and I didn't have the right words

to put my kind of smile on faces as I stood there
with little to say. Doors often closed.

I'd wonder at pedestrian crossings where people
stood in silent clusters waiting for lights to guide them.

I'd peer into a pale dictionary for sweetness
and when I needed shoes, I'd skirt round ways

of asking, how do you say that or I wish to be fitted
in style. I was a sinister consumer in an extravaganza

of street life and bulging waterways. It was all
clean and silent but it must have been that silence

that got me wanting to plant a fresh spring in my step.
And believe me, there were voices telling me

you have no right to enjoy yourself, but Mondays
wove into Fridays and Saturdays wove into Sundays

aa I walked about as free of guilt as a summer wisp.
That first day became decades.

If you stay on the road too long you miss the turn,
I'm told, and homeward bound and home

are only divided by dreary geography. I have
had my say so it's back to old objects and curiosity,

to cows and sheep that stare you in the face
without blinking. Even in white smoke,

knowledge takes time to work on the heart.
Another silence waits. We're leaving.

Home Ground

I'm back on home ground
where, these days, farmers
flaunt and preen in shorts
without fear of ridicule.
Daughters study Agriculture
and rock up on tractors while

partners and others drink carrot juice
or cappuccinos in convivial company
discussing wellness, bargains,
divorce options and good settlements.

It didn't use to be this way.
There were forms of incarceration
and torture that included
till death do us part, listening
to sermons on Sundays
or doing time in demon black bogs.

Between showers there were harvests
to make you so discombobulated
that crows, hovering and picking
in circles of their choice,
considered your carcass
if they hung about till cloud nine set in.

Mangy black cats
entrusted with rodent control
had it better.

CILL AODÁIN

And throughout all of those seasons,
down to this moment, it is the pull
of secrets hidden in blackthorn and bog

that call me back to where I can
breathe in roots – to where
there's hardly a sound – save for

the silence of swallows, the winnowing
of starlings, fog that tells us nothing or
foxes that build stealth into the fabric of time.

A blind poet – who dressed Cill Aodáin in
succulent red and black berries – found a way out
but never escaped. We have his word for it.

And the story goes that nature spirits rose up,
horrified at the grim mathematics of moods
when three men – now departed – tried to

hack down a reluctant blackthorn to build
a grotto in an open field. The blackthorn
survived but the tragic tale of the men sticks

in the throats of the those who dare to tell it.
The Oak, the Ash and the Thorn – firm
as stone-cold lips, stand guard against

the harsh message of Roman gods. Bells ring
and do what bells do in distant Kiltimagh.
Fathers, mothers, sons and daughters cry out

in Camden Town. Seasonal moons tell us what
we need to know. Farmers worry about silage
or the lie of the land and death cuts people adrift

to float away like feathers to places that
turn out right in the end. This is the order of things.
Life floats us back to where we began – to

my place – to my space and we don't wonder
at our luck. Words are raindrops that wait
their turn to enrich living and landscape and

I stroll by talkative streams thinking happy things
as my breathing grows softer and calmer – as I wait
to be transported to the silence of my ancestors.

Konrad

When Konrad, a young German,
came to Mayo in the seventies
he was heading for *Tír na nÓg,*
a Shangri-La without high tech.

Here, he could escape his own reflection,
far from the burden of his legacy.
He'd talked the talk, seen the pictures
and heard the music.

All he'd ever wanted was a remote cottage
by a stream, some cash for basics and
a bit of hillside for a goat and a few sheep.

He'd need a good garden to grow spuds,
carrots and onions like the locals did,
with herbs of allsorts and radishes too

and there'd be pool with lads in a cosy pub
and music round an open fire on Fridays.
He'd wanted to be at one with this banter,

to merge with the fragrance of hillside colour
where cows were content. He'd keep bees, and
on sunny days sell honey across the half-door

of his whitewashed cottage. Konrad was no quitter.
Years went by. His house shone. Flowers and fruit
grew rich and welcoming in his humming garden.

Neighbours would nod and when
he was away with dogs on the mountain,
they'd stop their cars to admire.

Tracksuits and trainers caught on.
Weedkiller was on everyone's lips.
Whitewash was frowned upon.
Flowers came from Amsterdam and
lawns were nurtured by pushy centre pages.

When he thought no one was looking
Konrad would go to the church
to light a candle – to weep a little
in his own language.
He was older now and hadn't been home
for a long time.
It was almost over as soon as it had begun.
Loneliness had to be learned.

The Road Out to the Coast

The road out to the coast might be wet and bumpy
but there's great buzz, lilt and illusion to be had
in cloud-nine scraggy light where, on a given day,

we are free to gad about in lovey-dovey rituals,
sing like billy-o in choirs of yippee-out-yonder
or whatever you're having yourself. On other days

there's silence that allows us to be quiet – to point
to nothing other than the roll of languid wavelets,
a caring breeze hanging about like a special friend

or linen-thin light signalling departure to an island.
And it's rumoured that a wobbly Angus calf grew
into a sturdy cow that kept the line alive on juicy slopes

not relished in Google guidebooks, maps and postcards.
In confidential undertones the trendy travel agent
tells the tourist that sheep don't wonder at visitors – that

children get carried away dreaming of far-off horizons
– that a high-pitched howl might be a black cat
under a rainbow
or a mischievous gale horsing about
in Ballina and beyond.

A Few Features

I know little other than
how to play a few tunes
said a satisfied woman
at the gable of her house
dressed in nothing correct
on a Sunday
at about the same time
as her child
swinging on a rusting gate
in the corner of a field
seems to scoff at progress and

when a lamb crosses a road
without looking left or right
a special antidote to craving
is being chartered and sketched.

A Walkabout in Killala

This morning, walking about with the breeze
spluttering rain on street life – on fugitive souls
and a seashore, I hear myself say, *it's only a shower.*

Door aren't numbered. Two women share an umbrella
and there's sunlight enough to backlight a kitten
in a cosy corner next to a flower pot. Over coffee

I think of the slave, Patrick, escaping from a wood
in Fochill and returning as a miracle worker when
voices called on him to light up a sense of something.

His death had a beginning but no end. Pilgrims
visit his church and holy well in Crosspatrick and
there are two churches in Killala to mirror his image.

Some scholars try to unravel the saint's history
and happy people say God created Guinness
to keep us singing from the same hymn sheet.

On the street again, with clouds still giggling down
willy wagtail raindrops falling like headless beads
on my hi-vis hoodie I'm loitering – my back to

the round tower – musing: a French Patrick would
be Patricius or Patrice and have spoken Irish with
an accent as sexy as a swallow in swanky circles, but,

rest assured, supernatural spirits on strings and armed
with big sticks would have been hovering in case a bout of
naughtiness got between Pat and Paradise.

Leave me my infidelity, I say, for I am as bamboozled
as a shamrock struggling to assert its identity in March.

Brown Bear and the Bus Driver

When a man left a public house in Belmullet
with a big brown bear as companion,
nobody batted an eyelid. To be fair,
the beast was wearing a hat. He was the one
that had left Dublin Zoo in a huff with no particular plan.

He'd ambled down to the bus stop
and waited for a double decker.
The driver, a kind man, helped him
clear the bus of passengers and
they headed west into the morning.
Brown went upstairs for a snooze after
a stop for a big fry and a pot of honey in Mullingar.

Crowds gathered and the police were called
but they backed off – the bear was resting
and the bus was a banger. When he woke,
the driver tuned into Midwest Radio and
handed him his harmonica for a stint of
tomfoolery that toned down as roads got bumpier.

It was late when they pulled up outside
The Broadhaven Bay Hotel in Belmullet.
Bear kept his head down and muttered,
I'm Charlie. Charlie Brown, while driver
skirted like a comma in search of a sentence.
Two single rooms please.
Right. Need any help with bags?
No. We're fine. Travelling light.
Right. Ye'll be ground floor. Stable and Stall.

After breakfast, they headed up town,
dropped into Áras Inis Gluaire Arts Centre

for coffee and got hired on the spot
for a medley of Erris country blues.

The town sprang to its feet. It rocked.
Taxis champed and queued – a judge
jumped out of her jumper and the
distant lighthouse gave off long-forgotten strobes.

Late next morning, with the wild sea settled
and the bus touched up in stripes of red and green,
they tuned their chords and hit off on a tour
of townland and town as far flung as Ballina
where they sold their story to the *Western People*
and the bus to the Tourist Board.

Job done. Driver left for Dublin. He was thirsty and
returned to the familiar. Brown headed for the Pyrenees.
He'd heard the bear population was in need of attention.

Holy Orders

There were druids, monks and
ascetics before our time.
Some heard light, passed on
and became saints. Most lived
in a routine of matins, vespers,
fine wines and tranquil gardens.

They had herbs and garlic
in their bones and could be heard
humming softly in purple fields.
They'd no need to screw up eyes
looking for playmates
or lie on their backs to tarnish
their torsos in holiday heat.

They'd amble to and from toil
when bells tolled and speak
when spoken to. Hills and valleys
joined with them in worship.
There was no panic in the fields.

If only we could down tools
and listen, we might hear them,
silent as ever – in their cells.

Begley and the Christmas Turkey

Begley bought a Christmas turkey
but balked at wringing its neck.
To summon up Dutch courage
he drank beer and washed down
oysters with herbal tea, but try
all he might, he could not find
a trace of killer instinct in his heart.

Even when his wife threatened
with cousins
and the Persian cat introduced
a note of silence
the hapless man could do no more
than watch the puzzled turkey strut.

He turned to media violence
for answers – beat himself up
with a huge stick – bought
a t-shirt with a gun on it –
visited an undertaker for advice
and rang an American friend
but the turkey had tasted his fear
and banked on a carefree New Year.

As a last resort, Begley opened
his front gate, closed his eyes
and ushered the turkey on to

the busy road. The Persian cat
intoned 'The Wheels on the Bus'.

His wife heard the crash, smiled and
turned up the heat. The driver wept.
Foxes gathered and hung about
for a bit. Begley shed bitter tears
and embraced the confused driver
before handing him his last few sedatives.

Heather

In some of Mayo's twinkling houses
modern families
have dinner in the evening
at teatime
and lunch in the afternoon
at dinnertime.

They discuss Netflix, fiddle playing
in donkey-and-cart days
when turf was turf
when planning permission
was for the birds
when Dubai was out foreign.

A daughter, Heather,
studying Heritage,
gets on to the topic
of medieval monasteries
along the River Moy
as her mother
on her way for a smoke
shrugs and mutters
something about
money being tight
and paying the oil bill.

Heather is heading for a talk
on Franciscan friaries
in the Ballina Arts Centre
while her dad gets on with
the laundry. They do Airbnb.

Take the Toyota. Tax
is due on the jeep
and if you're going
to the pub, be careful …
the lads in uniform might be out.

Billy the Busy Body

Even in Cong a dead man goes nowhere.
Billy was dead. Always a man of peace,
he lay quietly in his coffin and nobody,

not even his wife, could have guessed
he'd dreamt of shooting John Wayne.
You see he'd fancied Maureen O'Hara.

As an extra in *The Quiet Man*, he'd seen
redheads scattered all over the place, but
he knew they couldn't please like Maureen.

There was one low-set brunette with a few acres
who claimed she could sing soprano and skip
but she wore wellies and was mad about marijuana.

Billy did buy a gun but only shot a stuffed parrot
he'd picked up for a song in Shrule. He'd thought
of setting traps for Wayne but went for a few pints instead.

He was about to confess to his mother when he met
a Maureen after Mass and when she agreed to
dye her hair red, he – full of cupidity – fell to one knee.

In later years, Billy would often lean on his spade
and smile when pairs of starlings floated in unison
and perfect plumes languished in layers of cloud.

But emotions don't rest and, in maudlin times,
with the earth under his feet on fire and fragile,
he'd imagine a trip to Hollywood – but, as cash

for public transport was scarce, he considered walking at low tide – but, then again, there was Maureen, sheep, kids and things to keep a body busy.

A Love Song

In a remote County Mayo townland
an older woman feeds her goldfinch
on birdseed to keep it wholesome.

She prays the joyful mysteries of
the rosary – beseeching her god
of the sacred heart lamp to take

that bird to himself before he takes her.
She's a child again when she thinks
of their shared time and even if life

has been hit by modern use, her finch
has remained golden –
an old-school choir mistress and friend.

Deep End

Down a side road
next to a river
a weary old willow
drapes over a rock
and no one cares
not even those
who as children
had jumped off
at the deep end.

Most have forgotten
or want to forget
but the willow and rock
are still there.

John of the Priests of Ballyheane

John Mullowney, *Seán na Sagart,*
John of the Priests of Ballyheane
was one of a kind – a horse thief
and turncoat who'd saved his neck
by bounty hunting Catholic clergy
in those heartless Penal Law times.

You've sold your soul, Mullowney,
two fearless women mock him
in a shebeen – he steadies himself,
makes a rude gesture, bows and calls
for whiskey – for a pony and trap.

No madman has better ideas
on how to avoid heaven
than me, thought he
sitting
on
steps
or leaning on a military gate
while humming hymns to an
afterlife. *And those holy men*

are dropping like flies, he mused
tucking his wallet and dagger
under his pillow. He slept but

woke in panic and sweat – sick
at the thought of sharing a grave
with the remains of a decaying bishop.

Reward for a dead or captured bishop
one hundred pounds.
Reward for a dead or captured priest

twenty pounds.
Reward for a hedge school teacher or monk
ten pounds.

He might have written:
Dear Queen and Castlebar Sheriff,
I'll bring you dead clergy
by hook or by crook – and oh yes,
I am hot on their heels and
no chant can chime more glorious
than the sprinkle of cash
as reward for the thud of
a cleric crashing into eternity,
say I – the priest hunter of Ballyheane.

He met his death in the Partry Mountains
in pursuit of a Friar Burke
and was buried in Ballintubber
only to be dug up and flung into a lake.

The forgiving Friar Burke
returned him to the graveyard
but the bold gravediggers
faced him to the cold North
and not East to greet the rising sun.

An ancient ash has burst his headstone in two.
It might give us cause to wonder.

The Curate

I never met him but I heard tell
of the likeable curate who
lived up above in a big house.
Nighttime hours were dead hours.

He'd fancied a young novice
once
but they agreed to keep it
to themselves.
He'd never miss a card game or
a football match – he'd played
but gave up because he couldn't
share jokes and stuff with mates.

He wasn't supposed
to understand intimacies
and, anyway, he'd sworn
to offer up and sacrifice
for the honour and glory of God
but, then again,
his uncle in New York,
a canon of a kind, with
a girlfriend on the side,
was rich and
much loved for his preaching.

He'd like to have spent more time
with one of the teachers
and so would she but
the stern believers in the front pew
might not have liked it. They were
the backbone of the community
and clerical dancing wasn't allowed.

At One

Tom grew up listening to whispering water
telling tales of demon wind, holy wells
and spirits in shawls shrieking dread into children.

Death was present in doors banging, haws,
banshees, cats with five toes or moonbeams
shaping blackthorn into a matrix of fear and frenzy.

He'd tread lightly in layers of airy whim. Water
was half-magic, half-holy and bats half-blind
from ducking and diving in half-contrite light.

People were stranded between perfect rainbows
and imperfect saints. Stars were acknowledged
and time was meshed between birth and death.

Tom got lucky. He'd seen saints on pedestals
and dead scholars on pillars and plinths, so he
opted to stand shoulder to shoulder with an old ash

where he could idle away time – where dreams
smiled like sunflowers – where daisies assembled
and where he could be alone and at one.

THE FAN

An unhappy fan
at a Mayo match
up on the stand
on a warm day
out of the sun
in the shade where
it wasn't warm
and a man
would be better off
in the sun
as it didn't rain
and the football
was bad
as well as tickets
being dear
which meant
he'd not be
coming again
in a hurry
and neither
would his missus
as the seats
were not numbered
or comfortable
and kids had to
pay a fiver
for average stuff.

A Litany to a Celtic Tiger Housing Estate

Blessed be the names of homes:

Blessed be Anna Livia
Blessed be Babes in the Wood
Blessed be Brookside
Blessed be Chapel View
Blessed be Cois Trá
Blessed be Dewsbury
Blessed be Dewdrop
Blessed be Divorce House
Blessed be East Winds
Blessed be Fort Granite
Blessed be Hildegard
Blessed be Kandahar
Blessed be Laurel's Lodge.

Price is proof of value
cuckoo cuckoo.

Blessed be the woman
who stuck a note to a lamppost
requesting a call from
the man who had caught her eye
on that very same spot
the previous month.

Blessed be Liseau
Blessed be Maple Lodge
Blessed be Millenium House
Blessed be Nuns' Habits
Blessed be Pine Cottage

Blessed be the echo
of a lost childhood
when a mother refuses
all food and vomits
in the hope of finding
a trace of her image
in a cool mountain stream.

Blessed be Ringdong
Blessed be Roseville
Blessed be Sallybrook
Blessed be Sandy Ridge
Blessed be Sancta Maria
Blessed be The Pines
Blessed be Thornleigh
Blessed be The Willows.

Blessed be the grave of Jack the Bachelor
in the old village.

Blessed be door colours:
indoor outdoor
pub door to peace
back door to the terrace
front door to the tarmac
sliding door to the Joneses.

Price is proof of value
cuckoo cuckoo.

And knockers too
big and small knockers
knockers in blue
so many same knockers

with knock on effect
ah knock it off and
blessed be ye all … knockers.

A tidy man in row 7 to 588
2000 and after eight
jumped out his top window
into a straitjacket
in one turn
of his bank manager's key.

Cuckoo cuckoo.

Monday after work is golf
Tuesday after work is golf
Wednesday after Ophelia is golf
Thursday after work is golf
Friday after work is golf
Friday after Pat the Postman is golf
Saturday after breakfast is golf
Sunday afternoon is golf.

Blessed be my car only
Blessed be my drive only
Blessed be my car port only
Blessed be my car polish only
Blessed be my affairs only
Blessed be my patch only
Blessed be my bald patch only
Blessed be my skid marks only.

And the god in cleaning agents
and spirits
bless him above all.

In the Irish countryside
there are so many rows of houses
you could forget
to have a mind of your own.

North Sea Wind

Der Schimmel Reiter – a
dyke bailiff on a white horse
galloped headlong
into the howling North Sea
to rescue wife and child
to leave a lasting legend
of love and a dyke mystery
to ebb and flow and ebb and flow.

When hurricanes rip
across the flat land
of the North Sea coast
hardy black cattle lie low
like dots on canvas or
huddle along hedgerows
as if a chorus of critics.

In raging winds, trees
that shelter can kill
and words are cold comfort
on a wild afternoon
even if they do leave
a trail of conversation
in a *Gaststätte* after
dykes have been sealed
and sheds repaired.

Out on the mud flats
and up on the dunes
a storm lingers
like a poem waiting
to write itself.
Feral cats bask
in sun pockets,

a mongrel sniffs
at a washed-up shoe
and inside windows
neglected ones stew
on a wicked wish
that bolting lovers
get swallowed up
by all that's tidal
when promises of
a solid roof have
worn thin or
tired faces don't fit.

Some songs remain unsung
in the blue air of ebb and flow
but the tale of the *Schimmel Reiter*
lives on and on one note after another.

Gaststätte – Bar, Restaurant
Der Schimmel Reiter – The Rider on a White Horse

VIOLA

In a Hamburg U-Bahn carriage
a young woman supports

a musical instrument
bigger than a violin

and smaller than a cello.
It must be a viola – not that

I know much about music
but I feel this woman does.

She seems as refined as
a small white garden flower

exhaling rich pollen and
she looks as if she could see

staves, crotchets and quavers
transform the carriage into a

movement of symphony and sound.

When that Poet Passed On

A man of few words, that poet passed on
before his wife had time to comfort herself.

He'd bellowed from room to room, had dinner,
imbibed, grabbed his own chest,
wriggled a bit and croaked – leaving drafts,
tattered sketches and a two-sided face
to be sorted into spoken and unspoken piles.

My Soul Knows the Truth – his dog-eared work
lay open and as undisturbed as a forest leaf.
He'd highlighted: *If I were to reincarnate*
in an up-to-date carcass, would you, wife,
continue to worship me on my pedestal in sandals?

To get attention she'd used pills and distance, but
she had nowhere to go and every time she turned a corner
she bumped into his shadow.

In the days before his death he'd had a rendezvous
down an alleyway, met his agent by a white granary
and cancelled an opera evening for a major interview
on big time stuff: *Read my editorial on power and*
the alchemist in the city if you want to learn about demiurge.

On the strength of his belief, *life must be savoured,*
he moved in with a neighbour for a season or so, but
when she became expectant, he returned via the back door.

He'd meant well. That's why he came home.
I've come back to you, dearie. You are forgiven.
That woman down the street
just couldn't pick up on my undertones.

His wife wore black for a week or so
but soon took it off
when she saw the other woman looking
better than ever.
It was time for laughter and new ways of talking.

A Hard Landing

Any excuse and Hansi was in the air
out of sight and sound on cloud nine.
He'd whimper, *nein I won't sign.*
Another Shiraz bitte. Down below
on terra firma there were traps and
snares behind every smile. No escape.

Two women arrived at Terminal Two
to meet this one man. One woman
his wife. The other a lover. They
stood next to each other – both
blonde and unaware, but blonde
is not unusual at German airports.

The man, Hansi, looking forward
to his lover before his next flight,
floated through in American sweats
waving a heart-shaped pink balloon
he'd bought in Vegas. His wife,
full of quirky surprises and jest,
didn't visit her mother after all.

Hansi saw it all too late. There
was no way back up. The women
came at him from both sides and
grabbed at the balloon. He ducked.
The balloon burst. The women
tugged at him for a bit, got fed up
and rambled off for a cappuccino
and two generous slices of carrot cake.

One Forgettable Flight

On a flight from Prague to Berlin
I sat next to a very chubby gent
whose bulk spilled over the armrest
to lay claim to a third of my seat.
I know we were travelling economy
but I was paying above the odds
for a fraction of a seat and,
to add insult to injury, he'd
elbow me and snigger when
a picture he thought funny
popped up on his screen.
He asked me what I did for a bob
and when I told him I was a poet
he went quiet and muttered, *you*
must be an odd bod – he'd never
look at highfalutin' stuff in the air.
No sirree. Not me. I wondered
what Franz Kafka might have said.

That Undertaker's Clock

That vigilant clock above the undertaker's door
keeps an eagle eye on the drift and flux
of passing trade. Tick tock goes the clock

for smirking celibates, solitary couples,
pig farmers, talented dead, worshippers

of wobbling guts, screamers in silence,
dragons in drag, upholders of hypocrisy,

chancers in Bavarian dress and plenty of
pensioners planning paradise.

That undertaker's clock
ticks and sniggers.

Wealthy man, you imagined your finest wife
to be queen of country clobber – see her now
in her final shift with doors opening and closing softly.

The Grim Reaper out and about in the long grass
saw his chance – serendipity – bagged a bishop
in the arms of a Maria – a chimpanzee was

taken in, grilled, put through the wringer and more
till an acolyte swore he'd seen the cleric choke on
a chicken bone in a belfry. Grapevine gossip – perhaps

but he isn't the first and won't be the last. Miss Nice
who buys a daisy a day and cheese by the slice on
doctor's advice is closer to the high jump than she thinks.

A figure with cloven hooves, dressed to kill in lamb's
clothing and torrents of reddish hair, offers art to
the berserk, greedy or needy along dykes and ditches
where you'd hardly see a thing.

Motto: always choose a chunk of chicken to fit
your mouth and be sure to get swimming lessons
before crossing the great river in a topcoat.

Dead legends don't knock tick tock – or do they?
Ask Beelzebub, Pan, Faust, or Puck.
They'll be the ones messing about with balloons.

Symphonies from a Hamburg Street Café

Give me this city café discord any day – this
dystopian-book-feeling and sleeping-bag-sentiment.

In a blessed moment of wayward sounds, I'm
as free as a footless ankle sock at a hen party.

Atmosphere doesn't care about literary flair:
the singsong language of Maria Callas – the

supernatural buzz of busy mugs, blues
spoons on saucers, shrieks or tube music tirade.

An odd-looking man picks at a cake, coughs
without reserve or tissue almost upsetting me

and I settling. Morning, I say. Hello – his
voice melodic as if learning from children.

At another table over in a corner, there's a cluster
of mumsie kids. Stop bickering children. Please stop!

Ding-dong within. Breeze rustling without and in
the humdrum of notes and coins, *that will be … thank you*.

A delivery man drags a batch of fresh bread in layers of
trays. Scratch.

A young person reading is joined by a handsome admirer.
Nice.

An older woman on the phone stutters
and don't forget.

Cups crash – giggles – Jesus Maria.
Clean up.

My man is into his second helping.
There's a thud outside – an expletive.

If only I were a composer,
I'd be noting these chilli-ripe noises,
this song, symphony, air and grace –
this jingle of chant in daily use.

I'd hear wild witches in the city,
piano sounds in the rafters, pigeons

on a pylon or moments of heavy metal
and self-inflicted own goals.

I'd imagine an ancestor crying out
for the prattle of cash long before

days of bank manager hurdy-gurdy
or heads bulging with the flame of fame.

Some cafés sing and some don't.
This one does. Let's leave it at that.

Give me a Flat Any Day

When all the suburban flowers and
promises of streamlined sunshine
have vanished into glum, drear,
heavy red wine and hangovers,
I'm happy to be among bouquets
of trusted noises in my city flat.
I have no flowerbeds or walkways
to wallow in but I do have
the music of urgent footsteps
above me. I have a rich diet
of cautious cactus in a corner,
a cluster of cats on balconies
and daydreams of waddling ducks
on flip-flop feet that don't end up
in postcards. Next door there's a
faint chanting of Sunday service
and Pavarotti. I like it. I inhale
symphonies in the tone and brick
of these old walls. From another flat
I pick up on the colour of hysteria
with roots in war zones. I meet a man
on the stairs with a turned-up collar
and hesitant eyes of blue glass – he
hasn't got the language of here just yet.

Rows of regulated houses are designed
by colour blind men but I live in a flat
where I don't have to share hedgerows.

The Invisible String

In the city I sense life taking me by the hand
and setting me off on a journey with nothing
but a piece of invisible string to guide me.

I walk down to the Elbe like one that didn't care,
like others that appear not to care – like
the woman who said, *I can't explain things.*

Hamburg is home, whispered the Italian
who swore from a rooftop that
he'd return to his birthplace after death, and

I dream of a boy who ran so fast to the far horizon
that his mother lost sight of him and he of her.
They roamed this way and that without looking back.

I think of the poet, Wolfgang Borchert, who said,
Hamburg is more than cars, laughter of gulls, cranes
and dance music. It is endlessly more – it's our will to be.

We are strung together by shades of colour, fog and
fashion. That's what was going through my mind on
the U-Bahn to Lutterothstraße and up the stairs to my flat

and I thought, I've come a good way for this rich
emptiness
and that's not all – poetry
is the invisible string that takes me by the hand.

Lament to a Lost Suburb

A dark wet evening
in a ruptured suburb
I find myself nowhere
a rabbit in headlights
helpless in an illusion
on tattered pavements
with children cut off
from all caution as
frailer than frail
string over balconies
with no dreams worth
their salt to indulge in
air almost departed
and amen to a girl
beckoning my way
me inclined to think
behave as foreigner
even birds stay away
with nothing to be had
and little to report
not even a crime in
media dot.com and
few think about green
about despair they do
as I cruise in circles
navigation system kaputt
hoping I don't run out
of juice but I dare not ask
as I wouldn't know how
to begin in a lost suburb
of drear and lament.

An Ode to a Missing Manuscript

The gardener is not always the gardener
said the policeman doing his best
to calm the good lady
after her poetry manuscript had gone missing.

She'd fought off influenza and comfort
to complete it and she'd been
so proud and vocal in the café
where the pizzas and Americanos
were just about the best ever.
The place was awash with eager artists.

Her smug cat at the hall door had seen or
heard nothing, of course – typical tomcat.
She suspected the loose-fitting Bavarian
who couldn't write but who hung about
suggesting he'd sing, sketch or stay over.

She stopped to let her thoughts catch up.
Somewhere in a literary magazine
she'd Google a dead giveaway line
and she'd pounce and pin that plagiarist
to the trunk of the next lively breeze until
he, she or it coughed up to the chanting of chainsaws.

Her recent work had an edge to it, critics said.

Peril

When the dark beauty
was elevated by an angel
outside a café
she swore she'd
use her megaphone
to warn of pitfalls
in caprice and fancy
and she said
she'd stand at a theatre door
calling out: *beware*
of scooters scooting
along pavements
where innocent adults
stand kissing
with their eyes closed.

Pauli's Birthday

after a mini saga by Derek Seaward

In the greater scheme of things
it was a non-headline day
except Pauli was almost late
for his sixtieth birthday date.
He was usually late but
this time it was her turn.
With his sunglasses in
his top pocket, he was
well into his first Becks
when she swept in like a
Bond movie star in silhouette.
They embraced. Jaws dropped.
A youth surrendered his eyes
and alarms went off out of turn.

Happy Birthday, Dad. She sang like
her mother used to. On another day
he might have enjoyed it. He might.

TRAGIC FLAWS

When called to a fashionable fitting room
the manager came running. *Oh yes,*

it is a flaw good lady or gentleman.
No cover up, soul searching or tragedy.

Have a Carlsberg and pastry on me.
You see our house style is Danish.

Colourful as parrots we are, said
she or he humming note after note.

No doubt they'd have dressed nicely
in Hamlet's day in Denmark too.

His mummy wouldn't have done
her own shopping and neither would he.

He'd have been busy gallivanting
with Ophelia, drama and college or

he'd have brooded a bit – bogged down,
as he was, in layers of heaviness – only

seeing light on occasions. Mummy
would have seen to his washing and

kept him dandy in hose and codpiece
before wellness got to Castle Kronborg.

Hamlet's time was one of heroics
when revenge was bittersweet

and procrastination a tragic flaw
left to grumbling, *antic disposition*

or *flights of angels.* Epic was rampant
and the dead were endowed.

Even when his fated fiancée floated
with flowers in a singing stream,
he couldn't do his duty: axe his uncle
and be done with it. Hamlet is tragic

and flawed. Ophelia lives on in flair-tale
and in the names we give our children.

Out of the Dying Pan into the Pyre

in memory of poets Matthew Sweeney and John Hartley Williams

In Kreuzberg, Berlin, I was tormented
by the thunder of hoofbeats
on the pavement outside a coffin shop

on the same street as the theatre
where fellow rhymers would be reading
about death coming for poets.

Inside the window a skinny person
on a pert chair among slabs and urns
was poised like an addict aching for a

blast of incense. *In nomine Patris.*
Trying to pass myself as a grim reaper,
I pursed my lips flat on the glass pane

and licked a scythe into the condensation
but the man hardly gave me a glance
as if saying, *I am used to scared little men.*

Instead he seemed to check me for height
and lifetime at my disposal – his business
is constant and comes in off the street.

I was oscillating between life and half-life.
A red heart flashed like a piece of karma.
Reincarnation could be had on a recurring basis.

I'd be this way again after the event,
two hours older with a signed book
entitled *Death Comes for the Poets* – mortals

owned for a time by caretaker parents, partners,
relatives, then by an undertaker, by earth or flame.
Parts of me have died already. Life's the emasculator

ripping the young beast out of us. The poets
had been punctual but the books didn't arrive.
I had nothing signed to confirm that death came for poets

but was assured that words would enjoy a long and
healthy existence after the demise of the pen. We drank
to the mystique enshrined in language. Travelling home

to Hamburg by train, I slept dreaming of a journey
in a coffin ship from Ireland to America,
a time when death came for the hungry and nobody

cared about readings at The English Theatre in Berlin
or the shenanigans of a panicky poet
outside a funeral parlour. I woke. The train

slashed through towns and villages with
lights going out one by one on this strange planet
where we try to sing while poems are

being honed by slinking foxes in gathering fog,
by dozing cattle, crying babies or by
outlandish people from other places.

When I closed my eyes there were damp leaves
in shades of life and death and windows to the North Sea
casually deliberating on the shaping of another day.

From a Hauptbahnhof Café in Berlin

Here in a *Hauptbahnhof* café in Berlin
a tall bony man struggles at being present
with Becks Bier and Bismarck Herring.

He's not a drunk, more a like man
cut off from fantasy, waiting for a train
to elsewhere or a threadbare nowhere.

Did he ever stroke a cat or run away
from loyalty? His dark glasses rest
like veils covering up blood and flame.

If he's a dreamer, I must forgive but
his tight mouth seems lost to
lonely hearts research in a single room.

Perhaps he's a dark horse with
a mighty *Bundestag Frau* choking
on words that are almost her own

and he's the shadow of a ballet dancer
retreating to a pale other world or maybe
his wife's a pilgrim mother in a Berlin flat

where she longs for pallid widowhood.
She texts her dark daughter
recently made flesh and wearing that grim grin

of one who has finally got a lover:
I've got a partner – her prince
in training for perpetual isolation.

When one door closes, abstinence takes over.
I imagine him with credit card bonus points
offering tips on how to rescue a heart-never-young.

Their daughter, reconciled to hurt well done,
records the sound of constant silence.
All three are absorbed in giving little out.

A *Hauptbahnhof* café in Berlin can't be blamed for a sad face.

Die Gruene Meile Festival – Adelsdorf

for Johanna, Bernhard and Kerstin Blum

Like a stream of life meandering past shops, tents
and kiosks, *Die Gruene Meile* cut a swathe of emerald
through the town of Adelsdorf – a community singing

from the same hymn sheet. Bad advice and fevers
were on hold for a day. A sleeping dog opened one eye.
Cats and pigeons agreed to disagree and put themselves

on display – there were olive branches, words for the heart
and images for the eye. A policeman ambled along –
his cap askew. I read poetry in *Buecher Schmidt.*

A pastor and his wife sampled food and a youth gave
his eyes away. I'm sure the old longed for middle age
but didn't pretend. An aura hung over the town.

Sensations came when least expected. A granny had
a pizza. Jay wore a bushman's hat. Russia, Ireland
and Italy told their stories and left an international mark.

The World Cup was on every lip. Nobody got lost and
wives stuck to their own husbands for the day. An accordion
laid a trail of notes for children to follow. The Mayor paid

tribute to Kerstin. Dancers prepared to dance. A full moon
lay in waiting while Johanna tuned in to moods with her
eager camera on *Die Gruene Meile* – a mile in green and gold.

Electricity

after the Kitchen Power exhibition at The Museum of Country Life

Early morning back in the fifties
a man rushed into a doctor's surgery
in a terrible state about electricity.
I must be seeing things, Doc, he stammered.

The doctor became a little impatient.
Seeing things?
Yes, we got the electric light in yesterday
and the sight of herself shocked me.

The doctor sipped his tea contemplating
weight loss, a mild hangover,
Spanish holidays, a new car
and a radical art exhibition in Dublin.

The man had never taken much notice of his wife
but now one look at her in a fresh light
had him flummoxed. He knew of tragic outcomes
from The Western, Midwest, hearsay and all that.

A fine-looking woman she is and all.
She could easily leave me for another.
If only he could return to the old ways.
Even to dim the bulb might help a bit.

The doctor first suggested Irish dancing
but then his face lit up in an epiphany.
You could try putting a knot in the cable
and that might slow the current down.

Relieved, the man headed for the pub
but left after just one pint and began

picking primroses along the hedgerows
on his way home. A neighbour wondered

but the man smiled, happy to see where
he was going and what he had to do.

The Umpire

It might have been
an under-eighteens
Gaelic football match
but it was a final
and the supporters
along the sideline
were in no mood
for shenanigans.

Short of officials
a teenager in wellies
was appointed umpire
in a simple ceremony.

As the game got going
he began humming
a garbled version of
give peace a chance
to stymie trembling
and standard abuse.
He considered singing
standing upside down
to please the crowd but
thought it better not to.

When a low ball
dribbled into the net
he raised the green flag
without a whimper
and when one went
over the bar he hoisted
the white one manfully.

This is easy he whispered
to himself – happy
with the *him* he was
and he with his mind
on a tub of vanilla
but when he flagged
a point that wasn't
he heard sneers and
snarls as vicious as
blind dogs barking up
the wrong tree – but
when big-man-Eddie
bellowed, *I'll fix that*
effin gobflight in wellies,
skedaddle became a must.

To avoid bloodstains
the umpire legged it
in the direction of
a sign that read
Family Resource Centre
drop in any time
and he lost no time
in taking them up
on their offer.

Even now years later
whenever he sees
big-man-Eddie
on the footpath
he crosses over – just in case.

Annie

Remember Annie Brennan
of Aidan Street, Kiltimagh
who lived above and behind
her untitled shop. There was
little or no curiosity. Customers
stepped onto the concrete floor,
and she'd appear from within
wordless but respectful, quiet
as an undertaker's secret
hidden from passing trade.
There was nothing on the walls
to tell of history except
Gold Flake and John Player posters.

The floor was a sea of flour bags,
Indian meal and the solid counter
a galaxy of lollypops, allsorts,
eggs and sugar too. Brown and
white loaves stacked free and easy.

She might have dreamt of twirling
with Fred Astaire on sparkling bridges,
or she might even have enjoyed
whispering to blackbirds or listening
to trout jumping in the Pollagh river
on her late evening constitutional,
but the idea that people could count
footsteps to stay healthy
would have got her drowning in fits.

Grey hair was there to be tied back
in a bun. Teeth fell out in their own time
and sensible shoes were always flat.

Years went by. Her shop shut. Annie left us
but she lives on for those who remember her
shuffling in a navy apron or walking the road
to her homeplace in Killedan
in her Sunday coat after Twelve Mass.

CATTY'S CONUNDRUM AT SAMHAIN

My memory of Catty is distant but green
so it would be wilful of me not to shake up
thoughts half-hidden in fantasy and silence.

Anything but petite, this woman was bulky
with tufts of facial hair that kept children puzzled
and rumour had it she was a witch woman
who danced in patches of moonlight.

He husband would have been a thin man
who died under the watchful eye of jackdaws
or he might have left life in a careless puff

when Catty tripped and fell on him after a bit
of jig acting on drills. She might not have wept
but have sung *Cill Aodáin an Baile a bhfásann gath ní ann*

or maybe she did bawl into her pillow – slept
innocently among bats – his turf-cutting,
wood-splitting and spuds forgotten – but

in those pre-refrigeration times
Catty would have had a whiff on her hands.

Trees could weep all they wanted, briars cry
till the cows came home, but something
had to be done before feral cats and foxes

began to sniff – and besides, a postman
or stray nun might happen to pass that way.

The confused earth was tossing about,
losing its foothold – weeping – and thus

on a moonlit Samhain night with the wind
howling like hell, Catty shoved her donkey
between the shafts and headed for the river.

Some weary travellers – straggling home
from a riot of poteen, fearsome carry on
and ducking – thought they'd heard a
loud splash where the river ran by the graveyard.

One buck swore he'd heard a banshee baying
out of bushes. His friend was less sure:
On my oath I only heard Catty's sweet voice
and she keening to herself along the bog road.

Looking back, I see the whole townland
getting to its feet in dribs and drabs – to join
with Catty in a lullaby to the spirit of our ancestors.

This old lady dressed our world
up to the nines
in the fabric and voice of a maiden fox.

Cill Aodáin an Baile a bhfásann gath ní ann:
Killedan is the place where everything grows.

THREE WOMEN

for Patricia

Three strange ladies
dressed in black
emerged from a public house
late one afternoon
many years ago
and to my sister's surprise
they approached her
asking her to pass on regards
to our parents – flabbergasted
she said nothing but
to this day she wonders
who they might have been.

Famine

In famine, the dead were
never far from us.
Our children lay strewn
on doorsteps or along roadsides
and they were so far gone
that there was no chance
they could recover – even
if they did, a black stalk
lay in waiting
like a preying cat on a windowsill.

They couldn't drive suffering away.
Those potatoes that dug up
so clean and vibrant in a day,
diseased and fouled the fields
in a stream of pus before dawn

and some landlords cried out,
we'll give those peasants
nothing – for nothing
is what they've earned –
let them die. We'll put them
out on the roads
to compete with the grain trade
in a race for great ships.

Our families clawed
side by side
with snails and grubs
for the right to die
with grass and mud
between their teeth.

They did attack the drills
like flocks of crows
hoping to get to the food
before it festered, but
the rot beat them to the bite.
The famine god had
sickened every stalk
from the birthplace of
our farthest ancestor
to the common grave
of our youngest child.
That death – untalkative
and cold,
grabbed what it could.
What remained stayed
as it was or it was
cast aside or overboard.

The lanes they lived up
were left behind to fall
into disuse and silence

forgotten

except on occasions
when communities walk
the sad walk – to try
to greet the past face to face.

My Father's Day Out

It was late summer into autumn
in the seventies of the last century
with the wind slim as silk –
taking the heat out of things –

as my father appeared from above
robin-dapper in suit, collar and tie
like one not quite himself
but free as a whirlwind leaf – free

as a man can be in a Ford Escort Estate
and he on a sojourn of ten miles
to order feedstuff for winter stock.

You could ring the co-op. They deliver.
Oh hell no. I want to talk to the man.

Our recently installed telephone
was a riddle never to be solved.

Looking back now, I am glad of
those days when we were less mobile
at the tail end of the old world.

When the Concrete Cometh

for Aidan and Matthew Duffy

Given that the concrete cometh on time
there will be changes
that have little to do with a September moon
or the sojourn of the sun
but the path leading up to our front door
will be transformed by cement, water and sand.

For two days we'll be using the back door
and Cassie, our dog, will have to understand
that footprints can be permanent. Seasons
will come and go – we'll get tired and
pass on furniture, rows of books – even attitudes

but the day the concrete was poured – while
we stood looking from inside the window –
will live on as a feature and topic for a time.

That's the way it is
when things start
to settle and harden.

The Piper of Treenabontry

for Joe Byrne, Aghamore
and to the memory of piper, Joe Shannon, Chicago

They took their tunes with them
but the music refused to budge.
In Treenabontry I taste and smell
wind on the path the fairies crafted
when they chopped a corner off
Brennan's house – it had stood
on the track they'd worn to a frazzle
when transporting the music
and memory of the Shannon family
into posterity.

Before they'd left, melody tangled
about the house or hung carelessly
on hawthorn and briar – spirits danced
in moonlit splashes and stowed
treasured tunes in wistful wind,
dozing bog and landscape crannies.

Only those *little people* have
the language to tell us
where a musical note comes from,
how it lodges in the land,
in the heart of a departed family,
in a memory of a house.

Joe Shannon played the uilleann pipes
in Chicago. This was real – big
untainted sound – visible in loneliness,
choking fears, loss or in the smiles
it cloaked and covered up. It was
the stuff that held imagined fields,
fences, happiness and tears together.

The spirits of skinny streams
and tossing air knew this.
They held on to mossy paths,
untamed bushes, mists and forts
where they stashed away tunes
for home fires in strange places.

And when the new generation
learned a different way of talking,
old language lived on in melody.

I can see the thatched cottage,
wordless at first light. A mother
whispers to God at the cartshed door.
The anxious dog whimpers. Mist
falls on a bucket of hot coals
handed to a neighbour to conserve
the hope-giving fire for their return.

I see the loaded cart getting smaller
with every step of Doll, the old horse.
My mother stands weeping as her
cousins disappear into myth and legend.

Threenabontry, Kiltimagh, train, Cobh,
America robbing a townland of a widow,
Ellen Shannon and her young sons.
Only music dug in its heels and
refused to budge. It cut holes in hedges,
buried itself in watery rocks, wakes,
dewy rose bushes and railway tracks.

Joe had *the gift*
in the rough and tumble suburbs of Chicago:
a piper, baseball player and fireman.
His pipes – imitating rhythms
of blackberry clusters
of fire department sirens
of domestic sounds
of birds in the back garden
of being finally alone –
came to him by fate
like a harmonious fragment
when Patrick Hennelly – piper
and pipe maker from Mayo –
gave him his gift of pipes.
There were drones to be mastered,
children to be fed. His arms
would have been exhausted
from gathering food. Even
Odysseus in times of myth
must have cried out in frustration:
What are the kids up to, now, Penelope?
I can hear nothing in this light.

Francis O'Neill sang accolades
to his playing at The World Fair in 1934.
Joe tuned into the piping of
another left-handed piper, Patsy Touhy,
and off he went like a poet
trying to find rhythm in a poem – like
a mother building hope into
a prayer for a special intention.

John McFadden, the fiddler from Newport,
composed 'The Pleasures of Hope'
before Joe's time. Eddy Mullaney
handed him a set of Taylor Pipes
in the sixties. They unlocked squeals
of delight in Joe. He didn't ask who
he could play with. He just did.
Fiddler Johnny McGreevy lifted
his spirits. Defiant as robins in frost
they battered aside new waves
in their euphoria of reels and jigs.
They heard the far-off cuckoo
and the corncrake in the long meadow
in their country of home-from-home.

Music had found its mark. Pilgrims
descended on his kitchen. Joe
and Johnny recorded Noonday Feast
over cups of tea – word was out.
The young came running.
Piper Jim McGuire, Box player John Williams
and Liz Carroll, the fiddler,
threw their hats into the ring – Joe
gave them hope on nothing stronger than tea.

The Chieftains came and laid out a carpet.
They played with the big man and
acknowledged the *duine uasal* in him.
Willie Clancy School and Cork University
turned him out like new brooches
with awards and garlands – quiet as
his mother Ellen, he took it in his stride.

In later years, alone, he'd whistle
with birds in his back garden. They
responded. He took a pair of
cardinal birds into his home and
refused to bury them when they died.
They came to light in his basement.

Joe Shannon left as a boy in 1930
to answer the call to life in Chicago.
He went to the homeland of the dead in 2004.

The ghost in his pipes says it all.

Duine uasal: Gentleman.

West Wind

If you think the west wind
is confined to west Mayo
you're mistaken. It's not!

I dreaded cycling into it
on the Swinford to Bohola road
after school. Oh education!

I'd keep my head down – hardly
ever sing with cloud nine beyond me
and work-a-doodle-do in waiting.

How I longed to get waylaid.

Morning Train

February on an early morning train
from Dublin heading west
sweeping along in coffee and comfort.
We're on time. Houses are not modest
and tucked away like they used to be.
Some stand like great empty churches
in pomp and circumstance as if
expecting a crowd, but they feel hollow
and up for sale. Home's a commodity.
Hedges are wholesome, meadows greener
as slurry and silage have taken charge.
Turf is no longer cut and dogs don't freak.
A man with a handbag steps down at
Roscommon Station and a woman with
a toolkit on the platform could be Polish,
German, African – Irish even. Fashion is
the leveller that nips and tucks at individuality,
that makes us plainer and almost the same.

But fields were there before wellness or
slatted houses – even when famine raged
and no god cared. The memory of suffering
is deep in veins and crannies but the land

is slowly returning to its pagan roots
as it sails into light – as children, less sure
of their saints, hear other languages and
have classmates singing to stranger gods.

The Westport Train to , 1 July 2014

to my late mother on what would have been her birthday,
and to Dermot Healy who died last Friday

The sun has microfilmed – there's no need for tears.
My mother and Dermot Healy are dead. They never

met and died seven years apart but dead is dead as this
perfect day rises in me. I'm not in a tall building, but,

at least, I'm travelling first class by default. A mother
teaches her little son to be best in his class. I feel like

shouting: *Stop colouring in that ugly horse – there are*
three beauties out there in the meadow. Should I report

this woman for stifling vim and vigour – for
damage to a boy's head – for anti-social behaviour.

They are a unit contracted to each other. The boy
knows how to spell house and roof and suburbia.

He's learning to keep the lid on things – to cover up.
A completed construction might read: the roof is there

to keep you safe – under lock and key – out of
danger – out of harm's way – I'm your mother.

I'll pack you nicely and transfer love
into fear of big butterflies.

Stop looking out of the window, my son. Colour in the page
that says daddy's rich – that says money helps you not to look up.
Forget the stars. There are no storms on a page and
it's almost always summer. Keep a roof over your head.

Your mother means well.
She is indebted to you.

Jesus, Mary and Joseph meant well
in Paradise.

Allah meant well
in Paradise.

Dermot Healy meant well –
Dermot Healy did good …
he watched birds migrating.

My mother meant well –
my mother did good …
she watched me migrating.

Look out of the window, boy. Stop colouring in
for a moment. Look at those horses taking wing.
Imagine the moon ducking among the stars. Imagine
the dead catching up on games they'd forgotten
and, above all, don't forget
to build a skylight into your roof.

Graveside

With his back to a gravestone
in the old cemetery
in Castlebar, a man
told me that way back
in the good old days
it had taken three days
and three nights to
drive a steamroller
from Dublin to Castlebar.

When I queried him
about fuel consumption
he said they'd probably
had the Holy Spirit
sizzling and boiling
in a thingamajig attached.

When God Doesn't

Some good people in Mayo,
fed up with heavenly feedback,
have taken to writing emails
to the prince of darkness
hoping to get things moving.

One man had just finished a post
on a matter of utmost urgency
requesting Lucifer to intercede
with the Council on his behalf
when a voice sounding like God's
boomed out of an open window next
to the church and not far from his local.

When asked about his muttering and
sweating in public, he stammered he'd
just been to the sauna and confession,
and was on his way for his quota of pints.

Margaret Burke Sheridan

Margaret Burke Sheridan
might have worn
tracksuit bottoms in private
but in public
she'd be serene in the mood
and spirit of the time of day.

Morning blue
in sparkles.

Decent grey
in drizzle.

Orange courage
in sunlight.

Showtime deluxe
in ensemble.

Black night
in shutdown.

A prima donna and *adorable diva,*
La Sheridan lit up daylight for the day
and like a dawn chorus on a skyline,
she set her aura free
for us to imbibe in the wine
and earth of rounded Italian flair.

Twelve years long she stunned Puccini,
La Scala and Covent Garden,
then stopped to swap footlights
for a budget of bedsits and hotel suites.

Some swear it's a wisp of light or a bead of sun
they inhale when out sketching – others say no,

it's the strain and sparkle of Margherita coming
to uplift in great armfuls of wind, they taste.

Margaret Burke Sheridan can't be given back.
She's *Maggie from Mayo* in costume

on Main Street, Castle Street and up to The Mall
where she will remain. Just like that.

So let's tune in and walk about all ears – there's
song enough to go round – tone deaf is not an excuse.

The Beauty and the Priest

Relationship is exaggerated, insisted the cleric
comforting the beauty over a casual cup in
the judge's tent at the annual countywide showpiece.

He was corpulent, seemingly celibate and
had a caravan with curtains for downtime.
She sensed she was a poet in the making and,

as her mother loved Doctor Zhivago in furs,
she might well be part Russian. She was
learning to fly with her everyday demons.

Never touch them – said she to his offer
of a Jaffa cake – *which leaves two for me,*
giggled he, stroking his bumper baseline.

She made shapes with crumbs on the table,
and while he settled his sunglasses, she
lifted her lavish eyes, swallowed and sighed.

I'm writing a big book, he blurted, *and*
I play golf with a few friends on Fridays,
never once hinting at sacrifice or Sundays.

He was coming up with a cunning plan when
a swarthy trader, full of dark melancholy and
far cry from paid-up-parishioner approached.

She melted, waved a little and left. Crushed,
the cleric headed for the coast and opened
his curtains to let in what was left of outside.

PROUD CLIFFS

I try to imagine
the adrenaline rush
the Atlantic swell
must feel
when all pumped up
and pounding
it tries to fulfil
its dream of
being first
over the clifftop
like a pole vaulter
like a real number one
only to crash
land hard and
fade into pools
of its own
white sweat
in the orbit
of the turning moon.

The cliff might
be the benchmark
and bar but
swell is no quitter.
It will retreat
to gather itself
to piggyback pace
and momentum
in the flow and
rhythm of slipstream

even cheat a bit
in a fresh attempt
to tackle the beast
but proud cliffs
don't lower their
standards to please.

Wi-Fi Poaching

When you overhear a person in a Mac shop
enquiring about offers on milking stools

and if you later see them perched
outside a garage with a gadget or

looking shady in shrubbery, chances are
they are Wi-Fi poachers, freeloaders,

backpacking piggy-backers, cuckoos
relying on mother goodness to hatch an egg.

Even worse, they might be tuning into matters
intended for personal use or the confessional.

If only football or racing results were at stake,
you could live with it. But no, these people

read in the light of a neighbour's window to
save on electricity. Advice: have binoculars handy

and when sponger's expression builds like
a transgression, pull the plug on the router

and listen for screams of rage. Put a sign up:
try Morse, smoke signals, milk your own system,

knock on my door and allow me to introduce you
to my wireless parrot, Polly.

And what does that tell us? Nothing except
Polly is a parrot and it's unusual to see a person

milking a gadget in a dark corner next to a garage
after witching hour and not a spider in sight.

Covid Lockdown

I'm a spring tide going out,
an uncrowned berry on a bush,

a dreaming fox in a blurb
of moonsome dancing

with a string of stray sausages
tossed over one shoulder

and a free *faux pas* picking
at placebos dipped in fear.

My whispers shout – *it's me!*

Stars and days queue up
to consider me – isolated,

a nocturnal beast at bright time
with nothing better to do

than throw a spotlight on myself,
the unused actor pleading to play

the skeleton of a fairy queen
sneaking past a therapist's sofa.

Clapping and candles
don't tell the whole story.

An Ode to the Fully Jabbed

If you haven't been fully jabbed
you are nothing short of an unpicked rash

sniffing your own linen in public – you're
a backside boil on a slippery slope,

a weirdo out of work and don't give me
your funny stuff about boxing and quick jabs.

I wear my mask in bed when counting coins.
Nobody gets into my total isolation.

I wouldn't be seen near an unchartered dog –
they piddle on hospital lawns and ignore news.

I'm a stick in the mud in solitude, boosted
to the wishbone, weeping without suffering.

I was born in bed and I'll die in it. I distrust
dalliance with dewdrops and domestic fowl.

And what about bees? Get behind me
you buzzing transporters of contagion.

Your honey is the bearer of virus
cloaked in garden pods but not in mine.

I have destroyed all plant life, shot the dog, flung
the cat to the four winds and sprayed crusty flies.

I don't wear socks and, as I live in fear of frost,
I fight the urge to toss them to passing magpies.

I could wash them in virgin springs
to make them immune, wrap them

in herbs and spices and take them with me
to a perfect afterlife in virus-free paradise.

I know what you're at: gossiping in shops,
tell-tattling about my clinging

to tree trunks after dark and nibbling
at imaginary cabbage leaves in daylight.

I am of flesh and bone. The earth will proceed
with me – me alone. I have been fully jabbed.

Destiny Murphy

Unknown to each other, two men
arrived at a central station
to meet a woman of colour.
One of the men was very black
and a news reporter – the other
fully white with freckles
who'd come to be her driver.
She stepped down lightly
in fresh tone and blue rinse.
She liked colour – even
wore beige once but, here,
on a crowded platform,
a tiny Fiddlesticks Theatre badge
was her only identification.
She'd seemed too white
for one – too black for the other.
Puzzled, they shrugged and left
as she faded into her blue
and velvet silhouette – happy
to carry her own bags and
to fill her glass herself – but
with a name like Destiny Murphy,
what colour should she be
to please in public places or
to satisfy relatives with binoculars
looking down on her from high horses?

That Wayward Bursary

How can I go on, I cannot
Samuel Beckett pleaded
and I say:
how can I go on, I cannot
with that beast of a poem
strapped to my fragile back,
with my muse out there
where clouds shape horses
and all I want to do is
for me and the beast to visit
a sick sonnet at the zoo
before it's too late but
as long as my muse stays
out of reach, we won't
have a ghost of a chance
of getting to Dublin
to collect that Arts Council bursary.

UCG by Degrees

In four years of odd socks and hysteria,
I whistled my hair loose

smug as a young buck with an ear
for tragic flaws and an eye for

vowel shapes in Smokey Joe's.
Turnover hadn't become a football term

and seagulls never missed a match
or mismatch in Fahey's Field –

see you in The Cellar
and bring the lecture notes –

galloping as far as we could
from nine o'clock tutorials

we were the centre of the universe.
Imagine. I was completely college

till I bagged my belongings
but I still wear the profile well.

THE WALL

And when word was out that the
US President was on the lookout
for bricklayers to build a high wall
between America and Mexico
Murphy was up for it. One signpost
read 'This Way America' and Fox News
declared America to be great – so
wearing nothing but a donkey jacket,
our buck took his trowel and teapot
and headed off to pilgrim all the way
into America. It was sink or swim
hook, line and sinker. Finding his way
would be easy. He'd be guided by gulls
and the sound of the sun – and if hungry
he'd reach down and grab
the singing fish that almost got away.

There wasn't much happening at home.
His lady had left him so he was free
to walk on water. He'd heard tell of
a green card but when washed up, he'd
check in with Donald to see what could be done.

The Man had Only Wanted to Buy Rat Repellent

The man had only wanted to buy rat repellent
to deal with a big yellow-haired rodent
and his colony of rat-a-tat plague carriers
but the shops were out of stock across the land.

And besides, what chance had a caring citizen
on a mission to repel rats – when even
the slimiest of rat-a-tats was handed a gun at birth
to ensure that schools could be used as target practice?

The big rodent's rhetoric was sketchy
and his commands simple: *wrap mobiles*
in the colours of our flag,
wear a God Loves America smile
when peeling onions,
stand poised on street corners and in bars
with weapons trained on Mexican TV
and focused on shooting at a Chinese virus
without blinking.

Bad was a good word. Foreign was bad.
A true disciple stripped to the waist
in mud and mire in sniper attire
in case climate changers dropped fake news
on USA soil via satellite. Literature
in letterboxes, guns in the air and parachutes
on the ground prevented the moon aligning
with the Greta Thunberg alien gang and Communists.

Asia has released contagion to bring
America to its knees – with little effect,
the big yellow-haired mutant preached.
Large numbers, in rat-a-tat costume,

dosed with anti-dissident disinfectant
were immune, he assured them – and
there'd be multi-storey torture centres
with hanging parties, gratis, he promised.

Droves of cheerleaders with Alsatians
would line the streets to counter
Swedish conspiracies and Maoist fans
in fanatical sweaty bottoms and Coca Cola tops
when masquerading as Americans outside gun shops.

It would be gala. Hollywood. Back gardens
and church properties were welcomed as
burial grounds – some balconies too, and
all American blood spilled for the flag
would be blessed by God and sold in supermarkets
at a price even the poorest could afford, he swore.

Now I ask you:
what chance has a caring citizen in sweats
when rat repellent is always out of stock?

Innocence and Pretence

The footie match Sandringham v Port Melbourne
is about to begin and already edgy young blokes
are thumping each other on the blind side,
innocent as enemy gangs at a children's party.

The umpires have warmed up. The ball's in play.
The small crowd hiss and spark like snakes
under leaves except for the fat water carrier who
doesn't get drinks to players ahead of the lanky one

who skips in and out as if in need of attention.
The fat one seems to have settled for the honour
of wearing colours and getting the better of gravity
on lonely legs – a man half-stranded in dreams.

As I was leaving, Sandringham was well ahead
but Port Melbourne fans were very vocal,
not prepared to stay the way they were
as long as their impatience remained impatient.

A tone-setting woman kept shouting *come on Port*
looking this way and that for peer support, while
big men just shrugged, digging deeper into their pockets.

She tells another that her husband's memory is shot.
Acts strangely, he does. Doing things twice. Silly things.
A bit of a worry, even went to the dogs without money.

But she'll bring him his own set of footie results – tales
of autumn wind. Her game will go on without high flying
and innocence will remain innocent until pretence takes
over.

The Chanting of Hoofbeats

Sour grapes are not enough to light up the mind
in the darkening buzz tattle buzz
of the Chapel of Clay bar under a black moon.

Enter a flame of a dame, worn to the bone
by a history of wind, weed, fungus and
other bits and bobs knee deep in tommyrot.

A horsey type in weary tweed, fumes into a phone
as his children huddle next to Mummy
like unpicked potatoes in a sloppy wet field.

Two buckoos lash into beers on an open tab
and the same again Lady, swearing they'd
tackle mules, even if the sky turned upside down

and then there's that bony figure, cowering like
an empty thing ranting to shadows in feckless light,
while hoping to cast off the pulse of endless time.

An ageing gent in pinstripe and hornrims
looks shifty sharing a page with a young woman
who has one eye attached to her shoulder.

Granted it's not early but I'd imagine the best
is yet to come if that couple sidling in sidelong
is anything to go by. It would seem that

an Ave Maria Gratia Rioja – even sour grapes
might just be the thing to light up the mind
in this Chapel of Clay Hotel bar. All that's missing

is the chanting of hoofbeats.

THE EARLS DIDN'T RETURN

Nine years and more they'd fought
till there was little left apart from
skyline blurbs pointing to the coast,
crows flapping and scavenging dogs
snarling at trespassers in uniform.

There's a border in Ireland now
that began – some would say –
when O'Neill and O'Donnell
of Tyrone and Tyrconnell,
took flight from where the
blue horizon is swallowed up
by the feral Atlantic in Donegal.

In that September of 1607 – with
hope under lock and key – the
path to Rathmullan pier might
have been charged and fraught
but following it to a continental sun
from a remote Ulster hilltop
was like a door to a dungeon
and one-way ticket at full sail.

Kinsale lost and Mellifont signed
they'd have closed their eyes,
vowed to rise, ride the tide
and return triumphant with
a regiment of Spanish support.
And when the line was restored
and they were chieftains in the
cadence of their countryside,
it would be the Gaelic way again,
and no other – there'd be
bareback riders by the score,

a full moon for every castle window
and doors that opened to the heart.

Defiant yells can soften and words
are useful but when not needed
they haunt until man becomes dream
and dream festers into everything lost.

And now, on board in darkness
the chieftains would be quiet
thinking of horses – of Spain,
dripping trees and blue hills.
They'd be thinking of wives
and children left behind because
household was hearthstone,
habit, landscape and family.

The canker grew at home. Wind
tore at trees and sun did its best
to keep wilting Ulster warm.
Cattle were grateful for grass.
There were new battle cries
and drumbeats to other shades
of a Christian god. Land danced
to the tune and politics of plantation
while ancient flowers and plants
opened to strange, austere masters.

The O'Neill and O'Donnell clans
sailed away – maybe a bit afraid –
taking Gaelic rituals with them.
There was little left to hold them.
They'd done what they could,

often in darkness – trying to
make up rules as they went along.

In Flanders, France, Spain and Italy
they'd have lain awake dreaming
– in a bleary-eyed sort of way – of
smiling, shambled, green cottages
and resurgence on riverbanks.
Their hearts might have wondered
if this pounding would ever stop.
They'd have pleaded with Popes –
with legates and Spanish princes but
other agendas and the wounds of Kinsale
kept Ireland and the Earls at arm's length.

Yes, they were well cared for and died
with little fuss here, there or anywhere.
That's why we have songs of sorrow,
love, pain and loss. What else is there?

LITANY

When a man
left his mother
at a litany in Knock
to take a conference call
with angels
in his purring jeep
he was heading
in one direction.

Acknowledgements

I am indebted to magazines and online platforms where some of these poems have been published: *Cyphers; Skylight 47; Crannóg; The Blue Nib; Live Encounters; Agenda; The Fish Anthology; Tinteán*; The Poetry File; RTÉ Lyric FM; Galway Poetry Trail, NUI Galway Campus; *Southword; The Café Review; Dodging the Rain*; The Prep Walk – Decameron; Pendemic Poems; The Wild Word; World Poetry Almanac; Vox Galvia Poetry, *Galway Advertiser*; The Wombwell Rainbow; Competent But Unfitted – Booksie.com; Speakeasy, Skibbereen Co. Cork.

Special thanks to Werner Lewon for *Two Notes for Home* CD: a two-part radio documentary on my life and work.
To Joe Byrne of Midwest Radio for ongoing support and encouraging me to write 'The Piper of Treenabontry'.
To Denis J. Buckley, AISBL Brussels, for commissioning 'The Earls Didn't Return' which I first read at The Irish College in Leuven, March 2022.
'Out of the Dying Pan into the Pyre' was longlisted for Poetry Society National Poetry competition.
'Famine' was commissioned by Mayo Enterprise Board to commemorate *The Spirit of Place* in Swinford, County Mayo.
'UCG by Degrees' is included in The Galway Poetry Trail on NUIG campus.
'From A Hauptbahnhof Café in Berlin' was highly recommended for The Gregory O'Donoghue Poetry Prize.

About the Author

Terry McDonagh has returned to live in his native Cill Aodáin, Kiltimagh, County Mayo after more than thirty years in Hamburg. His poetry collections include: *The Road Out, A World Without Stone, Boxes, A Song for Joanna, Cill Aodáin and Nowhere Else, In the Light of Bridges – Hamburg Fragments, The Truth in Mustard, Ripple Effect, Echolocation, Lady Cassie Peregrina, Fourth Floor Flat.*

Terry taught literature at the University of Hamburg, and was Drama Director at The International School Hamburg. In 2017 he was Artistic Director of WestWords, Germany's first Irish literature festival in Hamburg. Founder of Pen and Ink Hamburg and Mayo. He is narrator and acting voice in 'All Points West', Sinead McClure's junior dramas for RTÉ. In *Twelve Strange Songs,* twelve of his poems have been put to music for voice and string quartet by the late composer Eberhard Reichel. He's been a regular contributor to *Hamburger Abendblatt* and has featured on German radio and TV on many occasions. He was chairperson of the Raftery Returns Arts Festival in Kiltimgh. In March 2022 he was Poet in Residence and Grand Marshal at the Saint Patrick's Day celebrations in Brussels.